Mastering Etsy - The Entrepreneurs Guide To Creating A Thriving Etsy Business

Adidas Wilson

Published by Adidas Wilson, 2018.

MASTERING ETSY - THE ENTREPRENEURS GUIDE TO CREATING A THRIVING ETSY BUSINESS

First edition. March 27, 2018.

Copyright © 2018 Adidas Wilson.

ISBN: 978-1393503224

Written by Adidas Wilson.

Disclaimer

THE AUTHOR HAS MADE every effort to ensure the accuracy of the information within this book was correct at time of publication. The author does not assume and hereby disclaims any liability to any party for any loss, damage, or disruption caused by errors or omissions, whether such errors or omissions result from accident, negligence, or any other cause.

Table of Contents

Introduction

Etsy is an online retail community just like eBay only that it focuses on vintage or handcrafted commodities. Most of the goods sold there are in the jewelry, arts, crafts, housewares, artisan candies, baked goods, or paper-goods categories. For an item to qualify as vintage it has to be at least 20 years old and can be anything from photos, costumes, housewares, jewelry, and clothing. Etsy provides a great avenue for you to sell your homemade goods—but that's not all. You can find a limitless number of items on Etsy that will help your home business. For instance, if you use The Happy Planner, Filofax, or Erin Condren to schedule and organize your life or business, there are downloadable stickers and inserts that you can buy and use in your planner. If you need promotional items that have your logo on them; there are a good number of Etsy sellers that can make custom swag for you. They will not only make coffee cups and pens, but also cosmetics, jewelry, bookmarks, and pretty much everything with your logo and name on them. For a very long time, a majority of artisans and craftsman sold their commodities at open markets, fairs, and on consignment. Although the Internet widened their market, most craftsmen did not want to go through the trouble of creating their own e-commerce platform, website, or credit card processor just to sell goods online. Sure, eBay and maybe other e-commerce DIY sites might have helped with the situation but Etsy offered a platform designed specifically for craftsman. Etsy makes it easy for each seller to create an online "shop" with total e-commerce capabilities with the easy-to-use setup wizard. It is a simple, affordable, fast, and convenient way of reaching customers. Creating an Etsy storefront will cost you $0.20 for every item listed. For instance, if you sell handmade baskets, and you list four of them (of the same kind), the cost will be 4 x $0.20 = $0.80. In addition, you will be charged a 3.5 % transaction fee. If you decide to use the "Direct Checkout" feature, you will be charged a 3% fee for each transaction. If you compare the total cost of creating a website that has a shopping cart and acquiring a merchant account (which also involves processing fees), Etsy is way cheaper. Decide what item you want to sell. If you deal in crafts, you might already have an idea of what you want to sell. You can sell multiple products. However, it is advisable to start with one type as you learn. Set up an Etsy account. The first step is coming up with a username. Make sure it represents your product and at the same time remains open in case you decide to expand your product line. Set up and stock your shop. When adding your products, remember that great photos and product descriptions are important. Price your items wisely too. Provide excellent customer service. You want the buyers to leave nice reviews. When a product is in demand, keep the supply steady to build a lucrative home-crafting business.

Chapter 1
A Successful Start on Etsy

Starting your first ever-online business can be frustrating; with learning new terminologies, concepts, and other things that seem so complex. To be fully prepared for the first few months, it is advisable to plan ahead and figure out how everything works before jumping in. If it is your first time setting up an Etsy online shop or you aspire to have one someday, these steps will guide you. Gather all the major building blocks in advance. This way, the shop opening process will be fast, easy and manageable. Prepare all-important things such as photos, your bank information, and item prices. Choosing a business name is not as easy as you might be misled to think. Sometimes you might come up with the perfect name for your business only to be told that it is not available when opening your shop. This can be disappointing but do not lose hope, go on and open your shop. If you encounter this setback, add your initials, location, "boutique" or "shop" at the end the name. Before you open your shop, you have the option of changing the name as many times as you want, until it feels right (go to Your Shop > Shop Name). However, after you have opened the shop, you are limited to changing the name just once. It is normal to have big goals and dreams for your shop. Creating a task list and strategies based on one huge long-term goal can burn you out. Instead, set smaller milestones that will lead you to attain your ultimate goal. Achieving these smaller milestones will encourage and keep you going. Make sure the milestones are small and realistic. When a buyer comes to shop at Etsy for a specific product, they will type certain phrases or words into the search bar. Put yourself in your customers' shoes. Which words or phrases are they likely to type while searching for your products? Brainstorm and come up with as many words and phrases as possible. After writing them all down, underline the strongest ones. Now go to the listings editor and incorporate those phrases and words into your item titles, product tags, and the beginning of your product descriptions. Each week check your stats to see which keywords are effective and remove those that are not. Your photos should be simple, illustrative, and sharp. Consider studying a little photography to learn which camera, setting, and angle will work for you. In this case, a lot of practice is needed until you get it right; so do not give up. You have definitely come across a shop that was so well designed and organized you felt like buying everything. Implement that into your Etsy shop. Encourage customers to buy multiple products and come back. Do not wait until everything is right—just start. Everyone has to start somewhere and grow from there, don't hold back, just do it.

Chapter 2
Common Photography Mistakes

Substandard product photography, be it overexposed images or blurry close-ups, can really hurt your online sales. The following five photography mistakes are very common among new online sellers. Learn how to avoid them. When the light is less than enough, your camera lengthens the exposure to try and compensate for that. The result may be a grainy or blurry image. Shoppers love a clear photo of the product they are buying. So even though you are selling outstanding goods, dimly lit photos will turn away potential customers. How to fix it: conduct your photography by a sunny window and also use a reflector (a piece of white poster board will do) to focus more light on the product and eliminate shadows. Sometimes when you are shooting indoors, you might be tempted to use the built-in flash in your camera to make things a little brighter. What you do not know is that flash can cause shadows, mess with the colors of your product, and create unflattering glares. How to fix it: when you want to shoot your items and there doesn't seem to be enough natural light, try using soft box lights or a light box to illuminate the product and avoid harsh glares. Out-of-focus photos portray un-professionalism and buyers will highly doubt the quality of your products if they are considering it. If they cannot see the photos clearly, it is unlikely they will make a purchase. How to fix it: play around with focus settings. A lot of digital cameras are prompted to create a new focal point when you hold the camera's shutter button halfway down. Likewise, for smartphones, you can tap the screen on the spot you want focused on before taking the shot. For close up photos where you need to bring out the details of an item or for small products like jewelry, enhance focus using the macro setting on digital cameras. It is usually represented with a flower symbol. Setting your camera on a stack of books or a tripod also makes for crispier photos. Too many props in a photo leave potential customers wondering what exactly is being sold. This can happen when shooting items in a context environment like a pillow on a bed. Although it helps buyers envision the product in their lives, it can be confusing. How to fix it: avoid backdrops and too many props as they can overwhelm shoppers. The item on sale should be the center of attention. If you are not sure, use a simple and solid backdrop to take photos of your product by itself. For you to sell your products, online buyers need to assess all the important details of the item from your photos. They should be able to tell the size, color, and other details. Otherwise, you will lose them. How to fix it: include photos taken from several angles in your listings. If there are damages, capture them as well. For items such as clothes, shoot them on a model for the shoppers to get a clear image. High quality photos and enough information will attract and keep customers.

Chapter 3
Choosing Your Camera and Equipment

The right equipment will help you get fantastic shots of your products. In this chapter, you will see the advantages and disadvantages of various cameras and learn about accessories that will make your photos stand out. You will come across four major types of cameras when shopping. Smartphone cameras are pretty good and they keep getting better. With a decent photography setup, good lighting, and of course practice, you can take great photos of your products with your mobile phone camera. Pros: smartphones are small and portable. They help you save time when you need to snap your products on the go. What's more, you can edit and list the photos wherever you are. Cons: unlike high quality cameras, smartphone cameras do not use a lens for optical zooming. If you zoom while taking photos with your phone, it will be low quality. Moreover, smartphone cameras are not the best for low-light environments. Compact/Point-and-Shoot Cameras come in a wide variety of styles. They can either be limited when it comes to manual settings or have fully automatic settings. Pros: they are small and portable. They are easy to use as they have more presets (built-in settings) automatic modes. They are cheaper than premium cameras. As long as a point-and-shoot camera has a macro setting and at least 10 megapixels, you can take decent photos. Cons: the automatic mode on a compact camera limits your control over the shots. Since these cameras also have built-in flashes, they may not be the best for product photography. Digital Single Lens Reflex (DSLR) Cameras have a lot of options for manual settings and interchangeable lenses. These expensive cameras are more complex than the point-to-shoot cameras and they take outstanding photos. Pros: These premium cameras are versatile. They are easy to use and take perfect pictures even in low light. Their large image sensors absorb more light resulting in larger pixel sizes and sharper images. Cons: they are a little expensive. They are bulky and not fun to carry around. For someone who does not know much about cameras, learning the manual settings can be a challenge. Instead of using a mirror, light just goes through the lens, then to the image sensor and the image is relay to the rear screen. Pros: They are light. They have more functions and manual capabilities. They might be easier to use for a beginner than DSLR cameras. Cons: a little pricier than compact and smartphone cameras. They have less functionality than DSLR cameras. Older models might not take great photos. With camera lenses, you can take crystal clear photos of your product. Always consider "minimum focusing distance" when buying a lens. A specialized macro-lens enhances your camera focus when the object is close. Tripods help you take a steady shot and are available for technically any camera type. Get one with extendable legs so you can adjust the height of your camera. While taking photos, pressing a button may cause the camera to move. A cable release or remote control takes care of this problem. Seamless Backdrops/Sweep are usually a fabric or long sheet of paper flowing from the wall to the floor, with no creases. The continuous background makes your products pop.

Lighting Tools
Good lighting is paramount for flattering features.
Bounce cards and reflectors
Soft box Lights
Light boxes and light tents
External flashes
Flash diffusers

Chapter 4
How to Shoot Etsy Products

Just because you are not a professional photographer or cannot access a photography studio does not mean that you can't have amazing photos. Use these tips to take great photos outdoors or create your own photography set up at home. Prepare for the shoot; know the various aspects that you are trying to capture on your products and how you can highlight them. This makes it easy to come up with an order for the session and choose the perfect equipment. Photo shoots can be draining and time consuming but shooting several items at once will speed up the process and create consistency. If a session goes well, note the time of day, date, lighting conditions, and weather so you can always replicate the conditions in your future shoots.

Gather Your Materials
Photo shoot Checklist
Essential

- Camera or smartphone
- Lighting (natural or artificial)
- Hard surface/Table
- Tripod
- Background

Recommended

- Light reflectors
- Shutter release cable
- Props

- Camera lenses
- Clips for securing background
- Back-ups: spare batteries, chargers, memory cards, etc.

1. Choose Your Background

Simple and orderly backgrounds draw attention to the product and not the surrounding. Clean light-colored walls, smooth fabrics, or seamless rolls of paper make for great backgrounds. Consistent backgrounds for all your shoots are also good for your brand and shop.

Using A Seamless Background

Hang your background material behind your product. You can hang it from a backdrop frame or attach it on a wall or cardboard. Let it flow down and extend it on your surface (table or floor), then place your object on it, a few inches from the curve.

Using Outdoors Backgrounds

Outdoor backgrounds enable you to portray the context of your commodities through lifestyle photos. Use outdoor photos for context and indoor shots to give customers a closer look.

1. Light Your Shot

Good lighting and good photography go hand in hand. Always avoid harsh light; camera flashes, a strong fluorescent bulb or direct sunlight.

Using Natural Light

Diffuse The Light: Use indirect sunlight. For outdoor shoots, a cloudy day ensures no harsh shadows. For indoor shoots, place your products several feet from the window. Take photos when you have plenty of light, but not too bright.

Use bounce cards: a bounce card focuses light on your product on cloudy days. Make your own DIY bounce cards if you do not have any.

Do not mix the light: do not mix artificial and natural light.

Using Artificial Light

Invest in box lights: three soft box lights are enough to illuminate your product.

For small items, use a tent or light box: a light tent or light box streamlines your shoots with consistent light source and background.

Be careful with flash: avoid using the built-in flash in your camera and opt for an external flash instead.

1. **Steady Your Shot**

Anchor Your Camera
Place your cameras on a solid surface or tripod stand because if you hold it with your hands you might move and cause blurry photos.

Use Autofocus
Turn on your camera's autofocus function for sharper images.

Be Careful With Slow Shutter Speeds
Slower shutter speed leads to blurry images especially in a low light environment.

Get the right Equipment
Use a macro-lens or shutter release cable to enhance focus.

1. **Frame Your Shot**

Choose The Position and Angle
How would you like to position your image? Do you want to take a vertical or horizontal shot? Using the "rule of thirds" will also guide you.

Eliminate Potential Distractions
If an object does not highlight your product, it should not show in the frame.

1. **Test Your Setup**

Take a few test shots and view them on a large monitor.

Chapter 5
How to Photograph Vintage Items

When all your products are unique, photographing them might become something you do not look forward to. Mia Graffam and Ali Arakawa learned this in 2013 when they created Fare Well Trading. To buy stock for their online vintage shop based in New York City, they went on buying trips and accumulated 50-80 items. To list their monthly haul, they needed to take about 400 photos. To make this possible, they required an elaborate photography set-up, complete with a backdrop, DSLR camera, and studio lights. The entire process was tedious. Mia says that it drove them crazy; setting up the studio, taking photos, transferring them to the computer for editing and posting, then breaking down for the studio production. They spent five months repeating that same process then decided to revise it. Go Mobile: the first step was doing away with the fancy photography equipment and resorted to a simpler approach. According to Ali, they realized that using a phone to take the photos was way faster. They now use natural light and iPhones to shoot their products in front of a blank wall or on a credenza. Ali says that being organized is very important. They usually photograph their products in bulk and spend approximately five minutes on each item. First, Ali explains, she places all the items on a table near the photography area. She examines and cleans each item-taking note of the details to highlight in her photos. She then takes one product at a time to the photography area. She shoots one photo with props and four detailed shots. Next, she moves it to another table and sits down to write listing descriptions. Focus on the details: for crisp, close-up shots, the partners use a cheap clip-on macro lens. Mia says that she ensures that she captures each product in various angles and documents all-important details. She goes on to say that if customers do not have a clear view of the product, they might not want it. Before starting a photography session, they examine vintage items for wear or damage and make it visible in the listing photos. Set the scene: Ali and Mia demonstrate to their customers how to use products they would not otherwise use in decoration. By use of thoughtful styling and various props, they make their products come to life. Ali says you do not have to use something for the specific purpose it was meant for. They could use an old ashtray for putting an air plant because not everyone is a smoker. Ali and Mia have shot, listed, and sold more than 1,700 vintage products since they started their business. Mia now lives in Nashville, Tennessee. Despite the fact that they do not stay in the same city, both of them still source, shoot, and list new items for their shop. To maintain consistency in Fare Well Trading, they both use their iPhones, similar backgrounds, and natural light to take photos. They list 10-35 products in their shop every week.

Chapter 6
How To Photograph Jewelry

Jennifer Vinje founded Anueva Jewelry in 2016. When she was starting out, product photography was her biggest problem. Her desire was to show customers, through the photos, that her jewelry was hand-made. However, every photo she shot made them look mass-produced. Her main photography equipment was a light box with artificial light. This eliminated shadows and the product ended up looking like it was from some big anonymous retailer. The photos felt inappropriate and did not match her brand. At some point she used woven backgrounds, which did not work, either, because the patterns distracted customers from seeing the details of her dangle earrings. Another thing, her brand has two contrasting styles; rough, organic pieces and sleek, modern pieces and she did not know how to represent them. Jennifer wanted her images to reflect her creative vision, so she analyzed the photos and decided on an action plan. First, Jennifer ditched the artificial light and began shooting in natural light. This way, the earthly quality of her handiwork was emphasized and it ignited the boutique impression she was looking for. Jennifer decided to conduct her photography sessions during the day (1-2 pm) near a window. She moves the piece, especially if there is a reflection in it until she finds a perfect location. Unless she is shooting an opal, Jennifer avoids direct sunlight. To make sure the sunlight reflects in the right direction, she has a white poster board. Jennifer picks settings very carefully. She no longer uses the woven backgrounds; instead, she makes sure the backgrounds fit every item's aesthetic. For sparkly pieces or bridal jewelry with diamond milling, a poster board on a table goes for a plain background. For the natural-looking pieces, a natural wood or wood grain table top works perfect to complement the piece. Jennifer aims at shooting with longer exposures using her DSLR camera. To achieve this, she uses a macro lens and a tripod. According to her, photographing an object when you are very close is a little tricky and even your own breathing can cause a blurry image. When she doesn't have a tripod, rapid exposures work for her. Learn the camera's manual settings: manual mode is better than automatic for Jennifer. She prefers an aperture of f/4.5 which focuses light on the piece of interest, hence a sharp image. The background appears blurred reducing the time she would use editing the photo. Beware of overexposure: even Photoshop will not help you if you overexpose the details on your pieces. Jennifer ensures that her images are not too bright by adjusting the shutter speed or ISO. Shoot raw files: using her DSLR camera, Jennifer uses a raw format as opposed to JPEG. A raw format will capture all of the image's data while JPEG compresses that information. Always edit: learn to remove blemishes from the photos and lighten the backgrounds. Jennifer uses Photoshop to edit her photos. The visual story of Jennifer's brand is now more compelling after making the necessary changes in her photography. Her customizable opal ring has become her bestseller. Other sellers seek her advice on photography and her buyers are comfortable spending $200-$6,000 on her pieces.

Chapter 7
How To Create Craft Supply Listings That Sell

Eye-catching photos and catchy writing quickly turn window-shoppers into buyers. Creating an irresistible listing is an art that requires mastering. The following tips are purposely for craft supplies. They will help you attract more customers and more sales in turn. Clients on Etsy and Etsy Studio cannot touch and feel your product, and so photos need to virtually communicate the details. When a shopper looks at a photo, they should tell what exactly is being sold, in what color and quantity, and how it is used. This is one of the lessons that owner of Lytha Studios, Erin Weik, has learned in her 23 years of being a business owner. Customers love photos that accurately represent textures, colors, and the scale of items. They will experience an unpleasant surprise when a product arrives in a different color than the one portrayed. Julie Collings is the owner of Vintage Handmade, a shop for vintage craft supplies. Because vintage products are usually not perfect (with rusting, wear, and tear), she makes sure to capture the imperfections in the photos. Cynthia Treen sells sewing kits from her shop, Cynthia Treen Studio. In her listing, she includes images of the completed project for customers to understand and visualize the end result. Adding props in photos may cause distractions and leave a customer wandering among the items in the photo is being sold. For vintage items, clean and uncluttered shots are the best. Whether you decide to use studio lighting or sunlight, craft supplies should be illuminated with bright and even light. Because natural light can be a little harsh, use indirect light. When using studio lighting, set up three soft box lights for the sides and above your product. For smaller craft supplies, use your camera's macro setting or a macro lens to snap up close photos. Your thumbnail is the first thing shoppers see when they check your listing. It should be clear, bright, and illustrate what you are selling. If you are selling small components in multiples, the photo should show a cluster. This depicts depth and various angles and sides of the item in a single compelling image. Write specific and succinct descriptions; long, flowery descriptions might not work with craft supplies; just skip to the point. The format should be easy to read and informative. You should answer general questions like what the item is and what is its use, material used, key measurements, color, available quantity, shipping time, among others. The following three areas of the listing will aid in SEO. Tags: The maximum is 13 tags. Remember to use keywords that shoppers are likely to use. Every title should start with words that best describe your item. Attributes: choose suitable characteristics from the drop-down menu so buyers can find your supplies. Never think of your listings as complete. Always go back and make improvements to make it even better.

Chapter 8
Product Photography Checklist

For your next photo shoot, this checklist is a great starting point. Every step is covered; from the equipment you will need to lighting and editing, this will help you entice more customers. Product photography can be tiresome and time-consuming, more so for sellers with a lot of new inventory and those that sell unique or vintage items. Schedule time to photograph several products at once. This makes the process more efficient. Consider the various details of your items that you want to highlight and how best you can capture them before beginning the shoot. The following are just a few:

- Studio shot – a shot of your item in front of a clean, plain backdrop by itself

- Detail shot – a close-up shot that focuses on the features of your product

- Size and scale shot – this photo should virtually communicate the size (how big or small) of your item.

- Lifestyle shot – your product in its natural habitat.

- Group shot – a photo of your wares together.

Gather your equipment: you will need the following equipment; depending on the setting of your shoot and the type of shot you want:

- Camera or smartphone

- Light box or soft box lights (for indoor shooting)

- Backdrop (clean wall or seamless paper)

- Tripod (a stack of books or any sturdy surface will do, to steady your camera)

- Light reflector (or anything to reflect light onto your item like a white poster board)

- Macro lens (for smaller objects and details)

- Remote control or shutter release cable (especially if you are your own model)

- Clips, clothespins or clear tape (for securing items or backdrop)

- Props (to convey scale or use)

Set up your backdrop: the background should ensure that your buyer's attention remains on your item and complement it.

- Get simple, uncluttered background; clean, light/ neutral-colored and seamless.

- For a seamless roll, be gentle and do not crease it.

- Place your item a few inches in front of the background curve.

- Secure your background with clips or tapes.

- Use consistent backgrounds (or just one) for all your items.

Light your product: good lighting is the most important thing if you want your shot to be beautiful and clear.

For indoors shoots:

- Conduct your shoot by your sunny window and use a sheer curtain to diffuse the light.

- If need be, use a reflector to illuminate your product more.

- In the absence of sunlight use soft box lights or a light box

- Do not use your camera's flash.

For outdoor shoots:

- Do it on overcast days
- Avoid direct sunlight

Steady your camera: this enhances sharpness.

- Use a tripod
- Use a shutter release cable or remote
- Take several test photos

Capture your shot: take as many photos as you need.

- Make use of the rule of thirds.
- If using a smartphone, don't zoom in to avoid blurry photos.
- Your item should be the star in the shot if you are using props.
- For smaller products or close-ups use a macro lens or the macro setting.
- Take photos from multiple angles.

Edit your photos: if you took great photos, editing is just a final touch.

- Crop the photos to eliminate too much white space.
- Use editing software such as Photoshop or Aviary.
- Do not use Instagram-type filters as they alter colors of the product.

Final step is to upload your photos.

Chapter 9

How To Market Your Business On YouTube

Posting a standalone video on YouTube can help promote your business. Unlike Snapchat videos and Instagram stories that expire after a short time, evergreen videos on YouTube are there to stay and can be used as a reference and even be distributed on any platform. You may include a FAQ video link on the about page of your Etsy shop or have a short DIY and share it on all social networks. Creating videos featuring your production process, your products, and help customers connect with you on a deeper level, bridging the gap that exists between small craft retail and the cold nature of online retail. YouTube videos also widen your market hence more customers. The following suggestions will help you make an amazing first video. If you are just starting your video channel, a quick introduction gives the viewers context. In a minute or two, tell them who you are, where you are based, what you sell, and the story of how your business came to be. Do not be afraid to share the video on all your social networks, encouraging your followers to subscribe to the channel. Take a step further and have this introduction video link in your press pitch emails. Consumers are more compelled to buy a handmade product more when they learn and respect the creative process. Capture the parts that make up your product in various stages. For instance, capture the entire knitting process of a hat from beginning to end. When you list a new product in your shop, consider posting a release video to generate a buzz and attract your customers' attention. Share relevant details about your product to spice things up a bit, share the story of what inspired its production or what is so special about it.

Any online seller who has been in the business long enough knows that very few shoppers read written FAQs and policies. Use the video as an opportunity to address a few common questions. Use interesting visuals and sound effects to keep them engaged. A video of your product being used in context will also show the function of the item clearly and allow customers to envision themselves using it. Do enough research on your target market to find out how buyers are likely to use the product. This will help you present your product perfectly and answer relevant questions. Original instructional videos will attract viewers and encourage social sharing. Think of content that complements your products and brand in general; for example, a "quick tips" series on maybe styling your pieces. Short "How To" is also well loved by viewers. Storyboarding is the primary element in shooting a tutorial video. It does not have to be complex; a simple listing of what will happen in the video is enough. The shorter the video; the better, speed up or trim long, boring steps. The video should be clear. Zoom in where necessary so viewers can properly see the finer details. Experiment a little with various styles and be keen on statistics to see how the videos are doing. Be true to yourself and your business in order to create compelling content.

Chapter 10
Keys to Successfully Selling on Etsy

All new sellers are faced with the question of how they can increase views and purchases on their Etsy shop. There is no secret shortcut but the keys below will do the job. Sell something that you love; you should love and believe in whatever you are selling. As a new seller, you probably have other commitments. If you sell what you love you will be motivated. Get inspired; what would you love to have but can't find it out there? Read lots of blogs and magazines to see what people are buying and wearing then check on Etsy. The aim is not to copy another seller but to inspire ideas. Do research; what is that great product that very few people (or none) are selling on Etsy? Bringing something different to the market will make you stand out. Get found; Usually, buyers stumble on your shop from a product listing through search. It could also been featured elsewhere. Having more items increases your chances of being found. How many items? What you sell is the determinant here. If your items are time-intensive and expensive then you will most likely stock fewer items. Take a look at shops that are successfully selling what you are selling. The number of items they have in stock should give you a rough idea. Start with what you have; even if you have only one item, go on and list it. Do not sit around waiting to build an inventory. Creating more merchandise and adding more products should be an ongoing goal, not a requirement for getting started. Looks are everything; captivating photos will attract shoppers from search results and even enable your product to be featured on Etsy and all over the Internet. Take the click ability test; Try searching for your product and evaluate the other products on the page. Which photo makes you want to click on it? Is it yours? If not, learn something from those that make you want to click on them. Bring your product to life; since a shopper can neither see nor touch your item, let your photos communicate all the details to them. Search suggestions; try to figure out what shoppers are searching for. Type your item into the search box with vintage, supplies, or handmade selected. The words and phrases that appear are customers' popular searches. Improve your chances; utilize all of your tags by entering popular phrases and keywords likely to be used by buyers. Let your titles contain a lot of accurate and descriptive terms. Bonus key, ship internationally, Sell all over the world; selling globally increases your chances of selling. Let more people find you. If you want to appear in searches by shoppers from other countries, make sure your product ships to their country (include the destination "Everywhere Else"). Do not let international shipping intimidate you. It is not difficult. On your shipping carrier's website, you will get the average rates for shipping "Everywhere Else". In conclusion, get rid of policies that are not working.

Chapter 11
Is Your Shop Optimized For Mobile?

E ver since Apple launched iPhone eight years ago, the world has seen a mobile revolution that has completely changed how humans interact with their environment. Mobile apps continue to become a huge part of day-to-day life. Mobile devices contribute to more than half of traffic to Etsy and shop owners are keenly watching. Tammy King from OurVintageBungalow realized that this is a trending source of traffic that she cannot overlook. She started visiting her shop using her phone as a buyer in order to see what they saw. Just as you take your shop image and branding seriously, you should do the same about your mobile presence. Going by mobile shop trends, chances are that shoppers come across your shop as they browse the Etsy app. The tips below, therefore, will help you make a great impression on shoppers. Shopping on a mobile device mostly involves discovering new products and shops as you browse. A shopper starts out the shopping journey on one device but ends it on another, according to the Group product Manager for Mobile at Etsy, Arpan Podduturi. It is likely that a shopper browses the app as they commute and then comes back later when they have decided to make a purchase. On Etsy, they may favorite a shop or save it for a later time. Enticing photos and a captivating about page will draw their attention. Looking at her shop in the Etsy app, owner of MenemshaJewelry, Menemsha Abeyasekera, knew that something needed to be done about the photos. Your first photo on every listing should communicate to a potential customer what the item is. Among the many things that a buyer is likely to see first is the photo; make it a good one. It should be of high impact and quality. The listing page space on a smaller device, like a phone, is way smaller than on a desktop display; use the small space wisely. Roy Stanfield who is a Senior Product Designer at Etsy gives insight on a method that he uses with his team to make design decisions. Consider the most important details of your product and list them. Your title should be brief and every crucial detail about your item should be at the top. That is the first thing a buyer will see. Mobile visits are increasing and they will continue to be, according to market trends. Mobile should be part of your workflow now, just as it is Tammy's. She advises that part of your everyday job should be making your shop viewable on the Etsy shop. Checking your mobile storefront regularly will help you make necessary changes. It, therefore, goes without saying that you must have the Etsy app on your phone. Shop Stats shows you how many of your views are from a mobile device. Monitoring and comparing trends lets you know whether or not your listings are drawing mobile shoppers. Check the stats after tweaking titles or images to see if there are changes. Experimenting, as always, will help you know what works and won't for your shop.

Chapter 12
How To Get Found In Search

Most Etsy sellers strive to be found in search by online shoppers. This is a problem that can be easily fixed with time and a little know-how. During the process, think like a buyer. Step 1: Include Attributes In Your Listing; every relevant attribute should be included in the listing. Choose the category that best suits your product in each listing. Depending on the selected category, you can add more attributes to the products like size, color, and whether it can make a great gift. Step 2: Brainstorm Keywords and Phrases; always start with keywords and phrases that the buyer is likely to type in while searching. All your tags, titles, and description should answer each of those questions. Etsy search bar could help you track what shoppers are searching. Type in your item in the search bar; the words that will show up in the drop-down are the words popularly searched by customers. Include the relevant ones in your listing. Try the same with any synonyms you can think of and good keywords that you can find in your listing's description. Do not repeat an attribute that is already on your listing in your 13 tags. Step 3: Apply Search Terms To Your Listings; work your list of keywords and phrases into your product listing. Create Powerful titles; your titles should be buyer-friendly, enticing and have meaningful terms that shoppers are likely to enter while searching. The most important search terms should be at the beginning of your listing. Just because you have your main category included in the title (like vintage, supplies) does not automatically increase your relevance in search for the said items. Nevertheless, it communicates to the shopper. Experiment with words in your title to see which one has a positive effect on your conversion rate.

Maximize your tags; use your keywords and phrases in all the available tags. Diversity matters; similar items should not be named exactly the same. Diversify to target many kinds of shoppers. Your most important terms should be in both your tags and titles. Check your statistics to track your results. The information will help you improve your tags, titles, and description. A lot of hits with no sales mean you are probably optimizing for the wrong keywords. If the search terms are yielding results, do not make major changes abruptly. According to Etsy search algorithm, when a shopper favorites, clicks, or purchases a product after coming across it on search, the listing's quality score improves. Encouraging shopper interaction will improve your listing quality. Clear product photographs make a shopper want to click for a closer look. Always double-check to see that your shipping profile is complete to accurately represent your processing times. Also, tell your story in the about section and shop policies. Look for people to help with search terms and improve your ranking.

Chapter 13
How to Market Your Business On Facebook

F acebook is the largest social media platform in the world, used by people of all generations. It is, therefore, a great place to find potential customers. It is wise to separate your personal Facebook account with a dedicated business page for your Etsy shop. In addition to being more professional, you will have Facebook analytics tools at your disposal. If you have a website or blog, add a link to the business page. Facebook gives you an avenue to easily talk to your audience about what you are selling. Posting your listings on Facebook enables readers to click through your items directly. When trying to promote a new product, interesting details will keep the posts from appearing like a spam billboard. Using Etsy social media tool to share, personalize your listings, and potential buyers will not see recommended products from other sellers. Draw attention to your Facebook page in an email to purchasers after they buy a product or even on branded materials like business cards. Offer an incentive while promoting the page. What will anyone gain when they follow you? Share different types of content. Use the rule of thirds; use a third of your content for shop announcements, promotion of new items, and sales. A third for business related topics; and a third for sharing useful bonus items like DIY recipes or items. You can also mix up the posts through formatting. Ensure that you experiment with every post format allowed on Facebook including photo carousels, slideshows, and videos. Do not be afraid to use Canvas, a computer program for combining video and still images to publish your story across social media. One great advantage for using Facebook is that videos play automatically as users scroll through the Newsfeed. When coming up with content ideas, always consider something that will connect with followers. Conversations with your readers let you understand the target audience, gauge interest in new products and generate ideas. When followers engage more with your content, they will see more of it in their Newsfeed. Set a posting schedule and plan your content in advance. A regular rhythm is better; for instance, once a week. Consistency will also help in image branding. All content related to your business should make sense as it pertains to your overall brand. The content may differ across platforms but it should all point to your brand. Do not confuse your personal account with your business page. Let all activity in the business page portray your brand's voice. The Facebook paid ad service helps you target your ads to a specific group of Facebook users. It is advisable to start with a small budget as you learn how it works. Let your posts be sweet and short. A caption should be one to three sentences. With a Facebook page you can see views, shares, and comments as well as analyze overall follower performance. On your Facebook page, you can share as much as you like about your business. Let shoppers know everything that is happening—especially new stuff.

Chapter 14
Every Etsy Seller Needs To Know About Sales Tax

E tsy has become a reputable, wholesome marketplace for people to sell their crafts. Anyone who is a seller on Etsy will tell you that, contrary to what many people may think, it is an extremely lucrative and thriving e-commerce system. It is a great opportunity for sellers to make crazy amounts of money. The sales volume at Etsy continues to grow consistently and in 2014, $2 billion passed through the site. Since making money is involved, tax payment becomes an essential topic. The issue of taxes does not have to be a headache unless you fail to organize yourself from the beginning. The following are important things about sales tax that you need to know as an Etsy seller. You need to plan for sales tax from the outset especially if your business is based in any one of the United States where the tax is imposed. Apply for and get a seller's permit (sales tax permit) in the states that your business has a huge presence for you to collect sales tax. Ensure that your tax-related income is separated from your Etsy profits and revenues at all times. This prevents you from accidentally spending the sales tax that you collect. When the time comes for you to file sales returns, it helps to know that the tax money is sitting somewhere waiting to be passed on to the tax authorities. Whether you want to collect sales tax on your Etsy sales or not is entirely your decision. Maybe collecting, processing, and remitting sales tax for very low sales does not make sense since the cost of the entire thing may be too expensive. As a seller, the responsibility and decision to collect taxes lies squarely on your shoulders. Etsy calculates your sales tax for you. From the customer's shipping address, it will figure out the sales tax for the area and include it in the total transaction cost. Your buyers will see the charges for transparency. To allow Etsy to do this, sellers are supposed to add the sales tax rate for every state in which they would like to collect sales tax. Your shop must be open to the public before you can add state sales tax. The tax rates format should always be in decimal. Etsy only does what you tell it to do as regards to the tax issue. Ensure the tax information is correct and be ready to take full responsibility for it. You can apply tax rates to the shipping costs. In some states, shipping charges have to be included in the taxable sum; others prefer to exclude them while others have a few conditions. This, also, is up to you. Filing and remittance is your job on Etsy as a seller, even though there are reporting tools that offer a detailed breakdown of all your transaction for a given period.

Chapter 15
How To Price Like A Pro

A few factors affect someone's decision to buy something online. Some people may spend hours browsing and researching, while others fix their eyes on an item's quality or convenience. Despite what any buyer considers, there is one factor that is common to all shoppers: price. A buyer wants to spend within a "reasonable range" and a seller wants to find that sweet spot—which is not easy to find. There are two complementary approaches that help you find the perfect price. Use one of your products for experiment. The entire thing is trial and error. Be ready with a Google Drive worksheet or Excel worksheet. Here, you will use the cost of materials, labor, time, and overhead expenses to get the price of your product. Fill your worksheet; in numbers, based on the amount you currently spend. Figure out what you can change to better your bottom line. Note, the materials used in the production of each item and the amount you spend on them. For craft supplies or vintage products, enter the price at the time of purchase. Experiment: try deleting one material. How does that affect your cost? Note the changes when you reduce the individual costs of your materials. Suppose you bought your supplies in wholesale or bulk, how would the costs change? Account overhead; create a list comprising of businesses expenses not directly tied to a specific product. This could be gas, rent for studio space, or purchase of equipment. Document these costs. To get the estimate overhead cost for each product, divide the costs by the number of products you already have or expect to have this year. Alter the number of products produced in a year or just delete any overhead expenditure that is not really necessary. Cover your labor; how long, in terms of hours, does each product take to be prepared for sale? How much should you pay yourself for each task? Do away with a task or reduce the time a certain step takes, does coupling tasks make the process more efficient? Make a pricing goal; think about the dreams you have for your business for the year. Do not just price for the present. Now that you know what you are spending, will your target customer be ready to pay for that rice? This second approach involves use of testing and research to determine a price then get down to figuring out how much you should spend to reach your pricing goal. Determine how your prices compare in the wider ecosystem of products available online, particularly on Etsy. Big box stores should not be your direct competition, but a point of reference because of the difference in the added value. Who will buy your product and for what occasion will they buy it? You can price higher for items meant for gifts because people can spend more for a thoughtful gift for their loved ones. After settling on a price that seems okay, ask for unbiased opinion from shoppers and fellow business owners. You can also experiment on prices. Your ideal and actual prices may look quite different after using these approaches; try to understand why. Go back to your worksheet and make more evaluations. Your prices will always be a work in progress.

Chapter 16
How To Sell Digital Downloads On Etsy

When Jenny Kun gave birth to her daughter, she created a few prints and hung them in the new nursery. One time, she was browsing on Pinterest, when she came across a digital download on Etsy and she was inspired. She decided to upload a few of her items and made a sale on her very first night. The Crown Prints, her Etsy shop was opened in August 2015. She has sold almost 5000 digital downloads ever since. What Jenny loves about selling digital downloads is the fact that customers get their purchase within minutes and she does not have to struggle with shipping. If you are contemplating setting up a new shop for selling digital items, these tips will help you. Listing your digital items on Etsy is similar to listing a physical product. The only exception is that you upload the file that a buyer receives when they make a purchase. After a shopper places an order, they can find the file on there downloads page. Among the items you can upload include, text files, audio, or image. You are not required to have special skills to list a digital item on Etsy but you need enough knowledge about design programs such as Adobe Illustrator so you can create files easily. Jenny says that Adobe Illustrator allows you to resize your files and it is a handy tool. If you already know how listing and selling works on Etsy then you should have no problem registering a digital file for the first time. There are, however, minor distinctions when pricing and photographing your digital items and the customer service expectations are also a bit different. Outstanding photography is a huge deal for an Etsy listing. Photographing your digital items will be even more challenging, because you need to make sure that buyers know what exactly is for sale. Your titles and tags should emphasize that the item on sale is a digital download. Jenny, for instance, found a technique that works for her. She prefers to set up her own props and frames at home and shoot her own digital items as opposed to using the mock-ups sold on Etsy. With digital products, you will not take trips to the post office or require storage space but sometimes more effort is needed in customer service. Sarah Norwood, who sells digital download lingerie patterns and hand-sewn lingerie, understands that her customers require more in-depth information than her lingerie shoppers. Sarah has a blog that helps her share more details. A YouTube channel could also serve the same purpose. Use your customers' questions to improve your service for future sells. Before selling your digital item, send it to different printers so you will know what your customers are getting. When pricing; you have to think of things like the time you put in each design and what you consider a reasonable profit to attain your price for single pieces and sets. Then add expenses to reach a final price. Selling digital downloads allows you to add more listings to your Etsy shop, reaching a different audience. For Jenny, it has helped her grow both as a designer and an artist.

Chapter 17

How To Find The Right Manufacturer For You

Your ambitions will most likely grow as your Etsy shop grows. Contracting with a production partner might help create new product lines and scale your business. When you conclude that it's time you used manufacturing you should focus on getting a partner that will align with the values and needs of your business. You have two options; find a manufacturer on your own or use Etsy Manufacturing, either way, there are important factors that you need to have in mind. The perfect production partner is one who will help you attain your goals without compromising your values and standards. Find a partner that suits your business needs in regard to turnaround time, skills, cost, equipment, and experience, among others. Using Etsy manufacturing marketplace to find a suitable partner for you allows you to filter available manufacturers based on the stage of your production process they are well skilled in. The production partners that you can currently find specialize in machining and fabrication, textiles, printing, , jewelry, and metalwork. More techniques will be available in the near future. Consult other creative entrepreneurs when searching for your production partner, especially those that have advanced their business using manufacturing assistance. They could share their experiences or refer you to partners. Moreover, join an Etsy team or visit your local economic development office to get referrals. Being prepared means having all the information you can receive about the accomplishments you hope to attain even before you reach out to a manufacturer. Giving all the necessary information to a potential partner helps them assess whether or not their workflow and materials will be a good fit for your line of products. When contacting a potential production partner, clearly introduce yourself; outline what you do and what you hope to get from the manufacturer. Share all the specifics such as the kind of product, the quantity you want, and quote your price for the services. Knowing exactly what you want eliminates the inconvenience of miscommunication. However, be ready to hear their ideas and suggestions since they are also experts. Ask questions, especially if you do not understand the terminology your potential manufacturer is using. Another suggestion, acquire knowledge about the process that your production partner is likely to use—it saves time and money. Prototypes or samples should always be part of the manufacturing agreement. It is the only way to assess the products' quality, and decide whether or not you will continue the relationship. The sample does not have to be perfect; you can always ask for changes. Jumping in without getting samples may cost you a lot of resources, leaving you frustrated. Make sure, also, that the partner shares your brand's values like using sustainable materials. Building trust is key if you want a successful relationship with your manufacturing partner. Make a point of meeting the team that will be producing the products, even if you have to travel far. It helps to physically see the quality and materials. Finding a production partner is a big step and if you find the perfect fit, the reward will be worth it.

Chapter 18
Become An Etsy Wholesale Seller

I f you want to reach a wider market or grow your business, then maybe it is time to consider the wholesale business. Etsy wholesale connects designers with retailers, giving you the opportunity to grow your brand, selling to over 20,000 retailers. The wholesale business does not operate on the same calendar as e-commerce so venturing into wholesale might help to balance the valleys and peaks of operating an online shop. Owners of Whispering Willow Soap, Wayne Parke, and Julie Gold, noted that wholesale contributed to the stabilizing income from their North Carolina-based business. According to Julie, though selling online is exciting and offers direct interaction with buyers, it gets seasonal at times. A wholesale business helps to make their income more consistent. Venturing into wholesale could also strengthen the business. Marie Foster is the owner of a jewelry shop, The Whirlwind. When she expanded into wholesale her Texas-based business became more organized and she became better at keeping track of inventory. Selling wholesale means exploring a new marketplace that has different rules, terminology, and calendars. Do your research before taking the plunge. Julia and Wayne first interacted with other wholesale sellers, joined wholesale groups on Facebook, in addition to reading a lot about wholesale selling. Wholesale does not work for everyone. There is an "Are You Ready For Wholesale Quiz" on Etsy to help you determine if your business is ready. Adjusting to the wholesale price is always a great deal. Usually, retailers expect to buy your products at half the retail price. This cannot be easy for new wholesale sellers. Marieke Jacobs, a bag designer, says it took her a year to finally dive into Etsy Wholesale selling and even longer to completely come to terms with the pricing. Marie Foster also says the adjustment was hard and she found the pricing offensive at first. However, when she realized the unique relationship that she shared with her retailer(s), she found that there are many benefits to have the joint business venture. To sell wholesale, you will have to analyze your costs even more keenly. Know all there is to know about your pricing. Get a large spreadsheet to determine the cost of production for each item. Know which products you need to discontinue or cut cost (or even not sell in wholesale). Knowing the cost helps you price properly to make a profit. If you are scared at the thought of selling your products for half the price on wholesale, then maybe your current prices are way too low. Marieke admits to making this common mistake with her retail price. Higher retail prices may mean lower sales but you could make a higher overall amount. When getting into wholesalers, sellers may decide to come up with new lines or products that would do well in wholesale. Some shop owners may start with one item they may think is well suited. Marie advises that you start slowly with those items that you can produce in large quantities and are already bestsellers. Before becoming a wholesaler ensure that your production process is streamlined, scalable, and manageable.

Chapter 19
How To Use Instagram Stories For Business

The new 'stories' feature on Instagram is quite interesting. Simply explained, it is a loop of videos or images that you share with your followers and they disappear after 24 hours of posting. Don't go crazy trying to come up with a big strategy. Since they are only live for a day, try to have fun while acting professional. Use the 'real time' feeling to your advantage. Since you cannot schedule the story in advance, share fun updates or behind the scenes. Show shoppers your items in use. Things do not have to be perfect, keep it natural. Introduce yourself. Show your face so people know who is behind your business. Utilize #Fridayintroductions on a regular post, add them to your story. Direct them somewhere. Show a sneak peak of; say, a new product, a new blog post or updated merchandise then maybe, tell them to get more information from the link on your bio. It will help keep your feed clean. Do not disorganized the look of your cohesive feed with an announcement or a sneaky peak. Share it in the story instead. Have a routine or share consistently. Share whatever special ritual you have with your followers. No makeup, no problem. You are human, just like everyone else. Your makeup does not have to be perfect for you to talk about business or say hi. If you choose to share about your personal life, don't go too far from your brand. So much content; use your time well. Do not overwhelm your followers with tons of videos and images every single day, unless you are doing something exceptional for maybe a day or two. Your Instagram stories should supplement your brand and feed. Your story might be the first thing someone sees about your brand. You are not in control. You have no say when it comes to social media trends. Even as you try to keep up with social media, work towards building an email list—that will always be yours.

How To Create and Add an Instagram Story

Creating:

From your homepage on Instagram, click on the encircled + on the top left. Take a photo or press and hold for a video. Hit the check mark. Your story is shared. Alternatively, swipe right and the screen will show up. To add videos or photos that were taken previously, use any of the above steps but pull down to open your media.

To add:

Repeat the above steps; how are Instagram and Snapchat Stories Similar? Being able to draw or add text to a video or image, and the ability to download and save videos and photos to your phone. You can either run through all stories or just select an individual story. On Instagram, you already have your audience. If your Instagram account is public, everyone can view your story. You can choose who replies to your story. You can take a story and post it on your regular feed. There are limited filters.

Chapter 20

How To Promote Your Etsy Store On Pinterest

Etsy is outranking all other sites on Pinterest by a wide margin. This is expected since their brand falls in line with the interests of Pinterest users. How can you use Etsy's success to your own benefit as a shop owner? You can use Pinterest to boost traffic and sales for your business. For better results, have a clear idea of what goal you want to attain by advertising your shop. There is no problem with having many goals, but it is better to have one main goal and then other secondary goals. Most Etsy shop owners should aim at getting click throughs from Pinterest. These click throughs lead to a purchase. It doesn't hurt to have many followers but that should not be the main objective—it is a "Vanity metric". Pinterest users are almost always interested in making a purchase, unlike users in other sites. You do not need an outrageous following to make a decent amount from Pinterest marketing. First, focus on how to promote your shop then you can go for other ideas. On Pinterest, your brand is the main event. Therefore, understand if and how your activities affect your brand. Image is very important and you only have one chance to make a first impression. Almost every Etsy seller spends a lot of time practicing their craft; they barely leave time to promote their products. Be realistic when deciding on how much time you will be able to commit. Check out these promotional activities that promise huge returns on invested time. It is advisable that your username be the same as that on Etsy. Branding requires consistency. You can either open a new account for business or convert your personal one. The features on the two account types are not different but the terms of use are. Your profile should be complete with an avatar (preferably the same as that on Etsy), your location and a link to your Etsy shop. While filling in the description, incorporate some keywords for SEO purposes but do it naturally. Remember you are doing it primarily for human buyers not search engines. You can borrow ideas from Etsy Top Sellers' profiles. Set up your Pinterest boards; the boards reflect your Etsy shop. They are like your shop sections on Etsy. More boards with fewer entries are better than fewer boards with too many pins. Since every board calls for its own separate description, think SEO and use this to your advantage. Ensure that your images are optimized for Pinterest. The first picture on your Etsy listing gets pinned more often, so it should be impeccable. Different content performs differently on various platforms; that is why your site should be optimized for Pinterest. Tall and skinny images are better than short fat ones. Your description must be appropriate for Pinterest, featuring a strong call-to-action. Build your audience on Pinterest. If you can afford it, advertise on Pinterest. Otherwise, promote your boards on other sites such as Tumblr and StoreWoot. Pin regularly in a schedule so that your audience is not overwhelmed. Another thing, join group boards and interact with other sellers.

Chapter 21
Shop Stats You Should Be Tracking

A re you the kind of seller who is hooked to their Shop Stats? It is normal for sellers to keep their eyes glued to their stats every day, sometimes several times a day. This can be unhealthy. Even when you are having a great, busy month, just a day of low favorites or views can dampen your mood. Unveiling new ways to watch your Shop Stats can reduce daily anxiety and remind you of the time you have put into the growth of your shop. The five stats below will help you focus on the long-term trends of your shop. The views to sales ratio are also known as the conversion rate. It is measured over a long period of time. For instance, check your conversion rate for January to June and compare it to the previous year six-month period. If last year you had 1000 views and two sales and this year you had 800 views and two sales, you might think that your shop is not doing well because of the decreased views; while in real sense, you are selling more items per view. Focus more on increasing sales than increasing views. First, make your tags accurate and descriptive so that the right audience lands on your listings. Eliminate unsuccessful keywords. Second, increase the chances of shoppers buying your item by answering as many questions as possible. You can know whether shoppers stay around when they discover your shop by checking out the "Traffic Sources on Etsy", part of your shop stats. Traffic from your About Page or Your Listings means you have someone's attention. It tells you that potential buyers are checking out your shop. Does your listing description make people want to visit more areas of your shop? If you sell complimentary items, link to other shop section or items from the listings description. Internal traffic is good but you need to learn about the external sources that drive shoppers to your shop. Whenever you represent your brand on Twitter, Pinterest, Facebook, or any other platform, it is an opportunity for a potential buyer to land in your shop. Unknown external referrers are an untapped potential source of traffic. When an unknown website or blog drives traffic to your shop, dig deeper to know where they featured any of your items. Thank them and ask if they would like to receive periodic email updates or newsletters of your shop. Keeping track of all external event-related traffic is impossible. Owner of Harp and Thistle Stitchery, Erin Flanagan, decided to register her events against her stats. She realized that, following an event; there was a huge spike in sales and traffic. Encouraging repeat business is a great method of increasing sales. Specials and coupons helps reward loyal customers and they are likely to buy from you again. Coupon performance may not be in Shop Stats (it is in your Order Item CSV) but it is useful in tracking. Which coupons are working best for your target audience? Coupons can be shared in Message To Buyers or by packaging them with orders.

Chapter 22

How To Market Your Business On Twitter

Twitter is a great avenue to appeal to influencers, reach a bigger audience, and create a deeper connection with your customers. Here, you will learn how to have a bigger following for your brand and get the most out of your tweets. Signing up on Twitter is simple. You only need to choose a username/handle and register. It is important that you use the name of your business for consistency in your brand; it will also be easier for fans and customers to find you. Feel free to add your Twitter handle and other social media accounts on your business cards or any other printed materials that you package in shipped orders—satisfied customers will be happy to follow you. Tweeting is a great opportunity to let customers hear your creative story and let them see the face behind the shop. Mix posts and photos from your blog (assuming you have one); with posts about promotions and new products. Interspersing helps to create an all round social presence and engages your followers. To create content, start by making a list of the kind of tweets you want to post over the next one-month. It could be general categories such as behind the scenes action or inspiration. It can also include specific stuff such as holiday promotions or the launch of something new. Interesting content should form a huge part of your posts, sprinkled with product promotions. This rule also applies for any automatically shared links from other social platforms. Followers will get bored if they do not get to know the person behind the tweets. After coming up with a complete list of ideas, plot the posts on a calendar. When you commit yourself in advance to a range of posts, you will find it easier to stay disciplined and find ideas, even when you are tired of posting. Tools like Buffer of Hootsuite allow you to schedule your tweets to post throughout the week or day for free. Twitter is a great tool for promoting your shop if you are willing to tap into a larger conversation. Find out what themes relate best to your brand and then figure out how that can fit to a broader conversation. Make use of hashtags and align your business with larger industry topics and trends. Twitter is a useful research tool when trying to find new wholesale buyers or considering promotional partnerships. Before working with any new promotional partner or blogger, check them out on Twitter to see who their followers are and how they engage them. Monitor the people who follow you, as well as finding collaborators and influencers. Use SocialRank (it is free) to analyze and organize your followers on both Twitter and Instagram. Bit.ly is another great analytics platform. It shortens links for you and tracks clicks on your shared tweets. Twitter Analytics, yet another great tool, gives in-depth data on your followers and those that interact with your tweets most. Remember to be yourself and show some personality.

Chapter 23
How To Craft A Memorable About Section

One time Holly Slade, Forbes staff writer, wanted a story on running a small home based business. She decided to look for shop owners to profile from Etsy. She specifically wanted a shop owner that had a minimum of three staff members. Holly was going through several about sections when she came across Bread and Badger, Amanda Siska's sandblasted drink ware shop. In the about section, Amanda lists her staff members and describes her workshop and this made her land the spot in Holly's published story, "Running a Startup From Home: The Good, The Bad and The Ugly." The About section is a platform to tell your shop's story. When it's captivating and informative, you can build a large customer's following. It might also open doors to unexpected opportunities like collaborations and press coverage. When Amanda was featured on Forbes, her traffic shot through the roof. A great about section tells a memorable story about how you started. Giving primary details like what inspired you, the business's milestones, and the evolution process of your shop allows shoppers and other readers to connect with you on a deeper level. Amanda, on Bread and Badger's about page, talks about her dream of becoming a tattoo artist. She then realized that glass engraving is a similar technique "without sterilization and possible regret," she says. Sean, her husband, left his job and helped her expand the business. When you run out of ideas, imagine explaining to an acquaintance or a new customer and write what comes to mind down. High-quality photos are a part of outstanding about sections. Take it as an opportunity to let your customers in on the behind-the-scenes of your business. Let them see photos of you practicing your craft. To attract press coverage, upload five or more professional, high quality, (minimum of 1400 pixels wide) and have a shop video. It shows readiness should the press come knocking. You can either hire a photographer or do the photo-shoot yourself. Highlight your unique production process, materials, and whatever else will make your business stand out. Amanda of Bread and Badger's, for example, tell shoppers about there sandblasting process, which she does with her husband in their garage. A shop video and photos help them tell this story in detail on their about section. The owners of Bure Bure Slippers, Inga and Kestas, make shoes and slippers from sheep's wool; and in their about section, they show the entire process, from when the sheep are grazing, to the final product which is footwear. Sharing detailed information and photos on your about page makes your business friendly and approachable. The Bread and Badger's about page has a smiling photo of Amanda and photos and names of her husband and the two staff members. There are also links to the business's website, Twitter, and Facebook accounts making it easy for shoppers to interact with the brand.

Chapter 24
What To Sell On Etsy

When shoppers are searching for something unique, they go to Etsy. It is a meeting point for small business owners and buyers who love craftsmanship, unique products, and maybe a personal connection. When you open an Etsy shop, you become part of an international community of fellow shop owners and shoppers. Maybe you want to open a shop on Etsy but do not really know what to sell. There are three kinds of items that you can sell; craft supplies, vintage items, and handmade goods. You can only be limited by your imagination. Take a moment to go through the site and discover the wide variety of creative items sold there. More original products sell a lot because shoppers from all over the globe turn to Etsy for interesting and one-of-a-kind products. A handmade product on Etsy is one that you have personally made or designed. You can either physically make the products yourself or design them and have an approved outside manufacturer help you produce them. The manufacturer must meet Etsy ethical manufacturing policies. Most sellers of handmade items on Etsy offer custom orders. Personalized products do really well on Etsy. If you choose the handmade category, know that creativity is key. Do a lot of research online, and particularly on Etsy, to bring your imagination to life. Katie Daniels owns Twig & Cone, an Etsy shop based in Illinois that sells ring dishes with pressed flowers. She started the business in 2016, but before that she ran a lucrative Etsy jewelry shop for about six years. She had an idea one day as she was making her jewelry: decoupage the leaf and flower remnants from the jewelry projects onto ceramic or glass. She searched all over for similar products but could not find any.

Vintage-loving buyers frequent Etsy. It is a place where Vintage experts and collectors get the opportunity to create vintage brands of their own. For an item to be vintage on Etsy, it should be 20 years old or more. Katrina Dunlap has a successful vintage shop on Etsy, Salvage House Vintage, which she started in 2008. Although she began by selling personal pieces, she has now made over 5000 sales. When sourcing vintage products, she goes for pieces that align with her personal style. Through trial-and-error, she has learned what shoppers like. Photography and styling are a big part of her success. She tries not to copy other sellers and stays true to her own style. Etsy shoppers are usually creative. They come to Etsy to search for materials and inspiration for whatever craft project they are working on. In the craft supplies category, the things you can sell include ingredients, tools, or materials for use in making handmade products. You do not have to make the craft supplies yourself. When Stacey Mika started her shop, Anastasia Marie, she was selling custom stationery but now sells supplies as well. Her highest selling supplies are those with a wide customer appeal. The craft is not the end product so you have to spark your buyer's creativity through the photos.

Questions to Consider

Do you enjoy it?

Is it trending?

Will it bring you income?

Can it grow?

Chapter 25
How To Get Traffic To Your Etsy Store

Getting traffic to your Etsy shop can be an uphill task and in most cases, fruitless. The reason is that it is not easy to measure the shopper sentiment and attain a sustainable traction at the start of the Etsy journey. The aim of this chapter is to offer a few steps and methods to frustrated Etsy sellers, and help them get traffic to their Etsy shops. Cross channel promotions include marketing, organic promotions, and advertisement on multiple channels. Put your products on YouTube, Instagram, Facebook, and Pinterest to build a comprehensive outlook for your items. Also, using this cross channel promotion method might help you attract interested shoppers on these platforms leading to higher sales. The following are to-dos to follow when using the cross platform strategy. YouTube: post your item in a conducive environment; where it is complimented and its working and needs are highlighted. For instance, if you are selling a blender show it in a kitchen. Show the easiness of use, its beauty and how worth of the customer's money, and time it is. Pinterest: pin images of your items with their prices. Join groups, create boards and pitch your item in a skillful manner. Be careful not to make a hard sell. Instagram: this is another image-centric network. Show your photos in a holistic manner. Consider the desires and trends of your target audience. On this platform, your personality and image quality are of significant importance. Choose a customer persona and appropriately pitch them your item. If possible, show someone using your product in its correct context. Influencer marketing involves getting an influencer to pitch your item to their followers. An influencer is someone that people listen to, especially when it comes to a product or service. Influencer marketing draws attention to your product even if, for a short time. It helps in boosting customer confidence in your item and you may enjoy a rapid increase in sales as your store grows. Radical and highly followed influencers obviously cost more. Do your best to strike a balance between your expectations and the expenses. Pitch your potential customers. To do this in a way that is neither vulgar nor too blunt, you need to write a great copy, target your desired audience, and post the right clicks. Store optimization will allow you to choose a target audience, understand your competition, and come up with a strategy to approach the market. This is the combined pitch of two items that complement one another. This strategy allows the two sellers to pitch each other's customers, coming up with a new marketing component. Co-branding helps you reach a new market, increase awareness, and boost sales without putting in extra effort. The two products should not be competitors. Utility marketing shapes itself around your customer's needs and requirements. Pitch something that your customers really need.

Utility marketing is useful in:

- Building your brand loyalty
- Interacting and informing your audience about your product line
- Establishing brand identity

This list is barely exhaustive and is subject to change from insights derived from customer and market analysis. Experiment consistently with a few ideas and methods so that you can understand your customers.

Chapter 26
Selling Accessories On Etsy

Accessories make it easy for shoppers to dress casually or try a new trend. In addition, they help shop owners on Etsy attract buyers with lightweight products that pose no trouble while shipping. There is no shortage of one-of-a-kind accessories, so how can you make yours stand out? Here are a few helpful tips. Truly unique items are a great way to attract buyers and increase your likelihood of being featured. Taylor Hunt, a merchandising specialist on Etsy, says that shoppers connect with unique accessories. Gabriella Cetrulo, another merchandising specialist, says that when she is looking for accessories to feature she goes for designs that are not likely to be found in many stores. Dikla Levsky, a textile designer, owns Dikla Levsky Design, an Etsy shop that she opened in 2012. She sells printed silk scarves and draws inspiration from various textile traditions and cultures. She then mixes them up with modern styles and colors. Engaging her customers boosts her confidence in her unique style. High quality images make you stand out in a saturated market. Even though you are not a professional photographer, you can still take amazing photos that draw attention to your products. Annie Bukhman had no idea that she wanted to be a handbag designer when she opened her shop, Gift Shop Brooklyn, on Etsy in 2011. She knew one thing though, good photos were important for the shop. She might not have been confident as a photographer but she definitely knew how she wanted her photos to be, and she used all the available resources and modeled her products. While editing, she makes sure the color does not differ too much with the real color of the product. When you show your accessories in context shoppers can imagine themselves wearing the items. Gabriella Cetrulo prefers to feature shops that shoot their items in natural, lifestyle photos. She says that if you sell a bracelet or a ring, you can photograph it on someone else's hand holding flowers or a cup of coffee. She goes on to suggest that natural light is better and also do not over-style your models. Dikla's photos feature models posing dynamically to capture the bold graphics of her scarves while portraying all the practical details. She did not just figure out her photography style in a day, it took time to find the specific one that captured her brand aesthetic in an interesting way. In her five photo spots, Dikla highlights the essential information of an item and reflects her brand. The photos are taken from different angles and show how the item can be worn. There are also close ups that show finer details like print and fabric details. In her photos, she tries to show the quality and have shoppers know what makes it unique. When tagging products, you need to figure out every possible way that a shopper can find your items. Remember to tag the color and color descriptions to attract shoppers that are looking for a specific color. Use Etsy Editors' Picks to get insight on the commonly used terms by shoppers.

Chapter 27
Choosing Your Etsy Shop Name

Creating a strong brand starts with selecting a shop name. The tips below will help you brainstorm and choose a business name. Inspiration for a shop name is all around you. Browse through businesses on Etsy and everywhere else and try to find out what you like or do not like about the names. Are they memorable? What do you feel when you see them? There are multiple categories of business names and these are the most popular ones: These names are more like a formula. It is usually a phrase/word that spikes a certain feeling or vibe used with a descriptive word that says what you sell; for example, Delirium Décor, Urban Cheesecraft, among others. Find a suggestive word that portrays your style. If you sell elegant items, then use a word with such a feeling. There are many benefits of using these kinds of names and one of them is that shoppers can immediately know what you sell. The downside to using these names is that it is hard to adapt if your items change. With abstract names, you have to be really creative and come up with a phrase or word that identifies your shop. They can be unique words (Wynne looks at foreign language words, names of animals and plants, etc to find inspiration) or use two words to create a unique name. Abstract names have the advantage of being unique to your business and are easy for shoppers to find. Using your name makes you flexible to expanding your product line. An eponymous Etsy shop remains unique to you and you can explore various aesthetics and products as the business grows. The main disadvantage is that a buyer will not immediately know what you are selling. Once you have made a list of exciting names, you need to do a little research. To check for your name's availability on Etsy, type it in while creating the shop and click "Check Availability". If it is not available, you can add "Design" or "Studio" to it. Search the name on Google to see if there are websites or businesses using it. Remember, you want your name to be unique so that shoppers can associate it with your brand. Talk to family or friends, preferably those in your target market and get their thoughts on your name. Etsy Teams are another great place that you can get feedback or advice. Know the law; be careful not to use a trademarked name. Consult your local trademark authority to avoid conflict. Use your Etsy shop name everywhere— on your blog; cover photo, and social media, for buyers to find you easily. Think globally, what do the words in your shop name mean when translated to other languages?

Make Your Etsy Shop Name Memorable

- It should be easy to spell and pronounce
- Take a shop name memory test
- Capitalize multiple words

Chapter 28
Selling Home Décor On Etsy

What makes you feel at home? Is it the familiarity, the people, the comfort, or just the little things? Etsy is usually among the top places shoppers visit when they are looking for something that will personalize their living environment. Custom pillows and vintage vases are a few of the many items that buyers purchase on Etsy, to help them create the homes they dream of. There are so many choices for shoppers on Etsy when it comes to home and living products, so how do you make yours unique? What common household problem can your item solve? When owners of Once Upon A Hive, Jason and Monica Coffman, moved from Texas to Colorado, their home needs did not remain the same. Their doormat, for example, could not combat the mud and snow in their new environment. Jason decided to make a mat that would cater to their needs; one that has wooden slats and holes. All their products are created to meet a need. A home is a personal space. Wise Etsy sellers know this public secret and incorporate a personal touch in their customer service. Jillian Carmine of Jillian Rene Décor is a reliable home expert to her clients and customers. She opened her shop in 2008 and has made over 2000 sales so far. She makes decorative pillows and her best part of the business is when she receives custom orders. Customers are happy to know that you are interested and ready to invest in their home goals. Lindsey O'Brien is an Etsy merchandising specialist and she knows the importance of product photos. She says that your photos are the first impression of your shop and it is a great opportunity to make shoppers visit the shop. According to her, the quality of a photo depends on the staging just as much as it does on the camera used. Shoppers should know the size of the item from the photo. It should also answer basic questions about the product. Keep practicing on photography. Shooting your items in context inspires shoppers and they can visualize the item in there home; even better, pair them with other relevant household items. If you are selling a serving tray, photograph it with a few dishes on it. It is images like these that engage shoppers and make them even more interested. Study design trends like Jillian does to help you create new lines as the seasons change. Even as you try to keep up, always figure out a way to be different and stay true to your signature styles. Utilize the freedom that comes with having your own shop (something that designers in larger companies do not have) to explore trends. Jason and Monica are usually very careful in running with new trends. You may spend a lot of money, time, and other resources only for the trend to change very quickly. Do not rush into every trend. Be simple and create beautiful and functional products. Engage more people on your blog and other social media platforms. This helps you stay in the loop, you might be an inspiration for a new item or an influential person might notice you.

Conclusion

The first shipping process is usually more of a guessing game: how are you supposed to pack a fragile order so it arrives safely? What is the reasonable amount to charge? A little anxiety is okay and very common among new sellers. However, the more you do it, the easier it becomes—with a little advice from experts, of course. The first step in determining the cost of postage; knowing your product's weight and dimensions, whether you are shipping around the globe or just across the country. A kitchen scale or any other digital scale will help you know the weight. If you do not have a scale, don't worry; use the one at the post office, estimate your item's weight by comparing with other household items or look for the average weight of similar items online. Shipping prices depend on "weight tiers". It would, therefore, help to have some shipping supplies ready so you can get the accurate weight when listing. When you are not sure, pad the estimate weight a little. If you add extra for packing, it is closer to the next weight tier and you can round up. Refunding excess postage is easy, not so much requesting more. Other times, a buyer will need a product urgently and even be willing to pay extra for express shipping. Enhance your listings by adding shipping upgrades so that your shoppers can have multiple shipping options. Clear communication throughout the process with your customer is just as important as your packaging. Be honest about how long preparation and processing of the order will take within your processing times. Your shop policies should be clear on whether or not you accept exchanges and returns. Explain who will pay for the shipping costs and also the return window length. An expert seller suggests having FAQs to address issues like cancellations, overnight shipping, and the case of a buyer giving the wrong address. Always update the policies and FAQs to cover more areas. A customer should know their item is en route when you ship it. This can be simply done by clicking on the "Mark as Shipped" option next to the relevant order and the buyer will be notified. If you can, provide tracking information. Do not panic when an order is lost or damaged in transit. It happens even to experts. Etsy makes it easy for you to resolve order challenges. Once an item sells, the next step is securely shipping the order. A few extra ingredients in the package, like a thank-you note or a packing slip, will seem more professional and the package will even look complete. Packing delicate items call for more care. In addition to writing "Do Not Bend" or "Fragile", double box the fragile item and fill that space between the two boxes with newspaper and packing peanuts to allow, "crash room". Also, leave at least two-inch of padding on every side of fragile goods in their container. Customize your own boxes for unusually sized items using a knife, cardboard, and a packing tape.

www.ingramcontent.com/pod-product-compliance
Lightning Source LLC
Chambersburg PA
CBHW071726170526
45165CB00005B/2167